SHAD HELMSTETTER, PH.D.

Best-Selling Author of
What to Say When You Talk to Your Self

A
60-Minute
Book™

NEGATIVE SELF-TALK

&

HOW TO CHANGE IT

Includes
The official "Guide to Changing Your Self-Talk"
from The Self-Talk Institute

Negative Self-Talk

and How to Change It

Shad Helmstetter, Ph.D.

Negative Self-Talk and How to Change It

Published by Park Avenue Press
362 Gulf Breeze Pkwy., #104
Gulf Breeze, FL 32561
©2019 by Shad Helmstetter. All rights reserved.

Includes the official "Guide to Changing Your Self-Talk"
©2019 by The Self-Talk Institute

Helmstetter, Shad
Negative Self-Talk and How to Change It

ISBN-978-0-9970861-8-8 (eBook format)
ISBN-978-0-9970861-9-5 (Print format)

A 60-Minute Book™

More Information — Less Time

    This book is designed to give you the maximum amount of information in the shortest effective reading time. The quality of the information is the same as you receive in a full-length book, but the key information is presented in a concise, condensed format.

About the Author

Shad Helmstetter, Ph.D., is the pioneering dean in the field of self-talk and personal growth. He has devoted more than thirty-five years to research and writing in this field. He is the author of more than twenty books, including the international best-seller *What to Say When You Talk to Your Self* and the recent *The Power of Neuroplasticity*. His books are published in more than 74 countries worldwide.

Dr. Helmstetter has appeared on over 1200 television and radio programs, including repeat appearances on Oprah Winfrey, ABC, NBC, CBS, and CNN News, and is a featured guest on top Internet blogs and YouTube programs.

Tools and Resources You Can Use:

To listen to Self-Talk audio sessions on many topics free for 30 days from the Self-Talk Institute:
www.SelfTalkPlus.com

For information on self-talk training, or how to become a Certified Self-Talk Trainer:
www.SelfTalkInstitute.com

For information on becoming a Certified Life Coach:
www.LifeCoachInstitute.com

To contact Dr. Shad Helmstetter, or to arrange for his appearance on interviews or blogs:
Email — shadhelmstetteroffice@gmail.com

Table of Contents

A Personal Note from the Author:

In these pages, I have brought together the most important discoveries on the subject of negative self-talk and how to change it, and its profound effect on our individual lives.

This book was written for people who are busy. (That means most of us.) We take less time today to relax and read and enjoy; we want to get right to the point, learn something useful, and move on. We want information we can use.

In the following pages, that's what you'll find— information that is up to date, highly useful, perhaps even life-changing—with a minimum of words to get the message across.

As you will read in the following pages, because of how the brain gets wired, the key to retention is repetition. Please feel free to reread more than once any information you want to keep forever.

Chapter One

The Message of this Book

There is no greater path you can walk,
no greater goal you can achieve,
and no greater purpose you can find,
than to live up to the promise
you were born to fulfill.

The purpose of this book is to give you all of the basics you should know about negative self-talk and how to change it.

I will begin with twelve key points that summarize this book:

1. All of us were 'programmed' from birth on—and we end up living out the programs we received.

2. From the moment you were born, everything you heard, everything you thought, and everything you said out loud or to yourself was temporarily recorded in your brain.

1

3. The messages you received that were repeated frequently were physically and chemically *wired* into your brain. We refer to those repeated messages as 'programs.' The more often those programs were repeated, the stronger they were wired into your brain.

4. It is estimated that during the first 18 years of your life—if you grew up in a reasonably positive home—as much as 77% of the programs you received were negative. Whatever those programs were, many of them are still with you today.

5. The part of the brain that stores the programs you received doesn't know the difference between something that is true and something that is false. The brain is designed to act on the strongest programs it receives as though they are *true*—whether they're true or not.

6. As much as 90% or more of your programs are unconscious, and are completely hidden from you.

7. Along with your genes and your experiences, *you are the result of the programs you received.*

8. Everything you believe, everything you think, everything you say, and everything you do is the result of the programs you received—both from others and from yourself.

9. Your self-talk, right now, is a replay of the programs you have that are the strongest.

10. Negative self-talk is the combined result of the negative programs you received from others, and those you gave to yourself. Most of them are unconscious.

11. Because of its neuroplasticity, your brain is designed to continually rewire itself throughout your lifetime.

12. If you have programs that are negative and working against you, you can change them. You can *rewire* them—replace them—with different, more positive, and more successful programs.

That is the message of this book.

Chapter Two

Negative Self-Talk

Negative self-talk is everywhere. We are in the middle of an epidemic of it, and it is getting worse. Negative self-talk is so widespread that I have even given it a name: *Negative Self-Talk Disorder* (which I will cover in Chapter Four).

Negative self-talk is:
- Anything you think or say that looks at something from a perspective of what *won't* work—instead of what *can* work.

- Anything you think or say that over-focuses on your *fears* instead of on your *strengths*.

- Anything you think or say about yourself that repeatedly focuses on faults or flaws instead of positive qualities.

- Anything you think or say that causes you to see your world as filled with problems instead of opportunities and positive choices.

- Anything you think or say that limits you from being or achieving anything that is real and possible.

- Anything you think or say that limits your belief in yourself or your future.

What Does Negative Self-Talk Sound Like?

Whether you say it out loud, or think it silently to yourself, it's easy to spot negative self-talk. Here are a few examples of what negative self-talk sounds like:

"Nothing ever goes right for me."

"I just know it won't work."

"It's going to be one of those days."

"Why even try?"

"The only luck I ever have is bad luck."

"I just can't do this."

"I'm so clumsy."

"I'm so stupid."

"I can never remember names."

"This just isn't one of my days."

"Everything I eat goes right to my waist."

"I can never get ahead."

"I'm no good at math."

"Life sucks!"

"I never know what to do."

"I'm at my wits' end."

"That's easy for you to say."

6

"My kids are driving me crazy."

"If only I were (smarter/taller/richer, etc., etc.)."

"I can't handle this."

"It's just no use."

"I don't have the talent."

"I'm just not creative."

"I just wasn't cut out for that."

"I never have enough money left over at the end of the month."

"I can never seem to get organized."

"I already know I won't like it."

"I never have enough time."

"I just don't have the patience for that."

"I'm too shy."

"I never know what to say."

"I don't have the energy I used to."

"I never win anything."

"Nobody likes me."

"Everything I touch turns to (bleep)!"

"I just can't seem to get anything done."

"That's impossible."

"There's just no way."

"I never get a break."

"Today just isn't my day."

And on, and on, and on . . .

Each time you repeat phrases like those, you are literally wiring your brain to believe that what you're saying is true about you.

Negative Self-Talk Sets You Up to Fail

Notice that in the examples of negative self-talk above, in each case, the self-talk predicts *failure*.

Negative self-talk is almost always self-defeating. It sets you up for failure; it anticipates failure; it *expects* failure, like it's a sure thing. So when you practice negative self-talk—even when you don't know you're doing it—you're literally wiring your brain to fail. And your brain will do just what it is wired to do.

Negative Self-Talk is Harmful

Talking or thinking in a negative way might sound harmless, but it isn't. When you say it or think it, your self-talk is literally being recorded in your brain.

9

That's not good, because whether you meant it or not, if you repeat something in the negative often enough, your brain wires it in—and thinks it's *true*. And when your brain thinks it's true, it *becomes* true for you—even though it wasn't true in the first place.

Imagine what negative self-talk (which your brain will accept as truth) can do to your health, your family, your job, your finances, your goals, your peace of mind, your future, and every important area of your life.

Negative Self-Talk is a Habit

Occasional negative thinking can be a general 'down' attitude that is brought on by bad news, depression, or anxiety. But negative self-talk itself becomes a *habit*. Unless you do something about it, it grows, and, in time, stays with you. And the more you practice the habit, the stronger the habit becomes.

In time, with practice, occasional negative thinking turns into full-time negative self-talk. It becomes an accepted, 'normal' way to think. And that ends up affecting everything else about you—from how well you get through a day, to the direction of your life.

The important key here is, we're not born to think negatively—we *learn* to think that way.

Chapter Three

Where Negative Self-Talk Begins

Most of us have had the opportunity to visit the newborn nursery in a hospital. It's that wonderful place where we first visit precious little infants just after they are born.

In the newborn nursery, we usually observe the infants through a viewing window. There, on the other side of the window, snuggled in their little bassinets, we see those remarkable miracles of life.

Imagine looking in on a couple of those infants right now. They are amazing! If they're awake, and their eyes are open, we can see them looking out into the world for the first time, as though they are searching for that incredible life they were born to live.

When we look into the eyes of those infants, what we see is *unlimited opportunity and possibility*. They have their entire lives in front of them. Their potential is infinite. It is clear that each of those infants was born to succeed. *No one* is born to fail. In fact, everything about those little infants is designed to help each of them reach their highest potential.

Then, even as they leave the warm, comfortable safety and security of their birthing bassinet, and then a short stay in a hospital room, the first moments of the infant's programming begins. From the mother's first words, to the television screen in the corner of the room, the messages begin to come in.

During the next eighteen years of their lives, each of those children, if they grow up in a reasonably positive home, will be told *'No,'* or what he or she *cannot* do, or what will *not* work for them, an estimated *148,000 times!* Along with that, there will be thousands more messages that tell the child who they are, and what to believe about the world around them.

To the child's brain, whatever they experience, or are told often enough, begins to form the picture of who that child believes himself or herself to be, and what is 'true' about anything. Almost everything they think will be governed by the repeated programs they receive.

It doesn't make any difference if the programs they receive are actually true or not. With enough repetition, those programs become *true* in the child's brain.

Here's an example. Let's say that, instead of being born, brought home, and raised as you were, you had been kidnapped as a small infant and taken to a different home somewhere and raised by different parents in a different part of the world and brought up in a country that was an enemy of your birth country.

Instead of being 'you,' with the name, and the family and the friends and the education and the experience and the beliefs you have now, you would be the product of an entirely different environment. You would still be 'you,' genetically, but everything else about 'you' would be different. Your beliefs about almost everything—your faith, your ideology, your habits, the way you dress, your attitudes, your work, your relationships, your goals, your future— virtually everything about you would be different.

In fact, if that had actually happened, you could even view the person you are in your real life today as an enemy—and you could think and believe the *opposite* of almost everything you think and believe today.

How could that be? It is simply the result of the fact that while we are all born to excel, and reach our full potential, with our whole lives in front of us, something happens to interrupt that process. What happens next is that *the programs we receive* end up forming what we believe, and what we think about everything. Our programs tell us who we are, and even what we will—or will *not* do—with our lives.

An Experiment About Success and Failure

To make this clear, we're going to do an experiment. It works like this:

First, think of someone you know, or know of, whom you would consider to be a truly 'successful' person. I don't mean just financially successful, but successful in their *life*. This would be someone whose life is working. Someone who is living a life that is fulfilled, and always moving upwards. It would probably be someone you would like to spend time with, or emulate and learn from.

Take a moment and think of a person you would choose who best fits the description of "*My most successful person.*" It could be someone who is living, or someone who isn't. But whoever it is, get a picture of that person in your mind now, so you can see them clearly.

With the picture of that wonderfully 'successful' person in your mind, imagine that she or he is actually there with you now and is standing off to the right of you. For the moment, we'll just ask that person to stand there—while we add someone else to our experiment.

To do that, I would like you to now think of someone you would call the *least* successful person you know. This would be someone you know, or know of, who is 'failing' at life.

When I think of the least successful person I know, I see the picture of a young kid who left home because of drug use when he was seventeen years old, and his parents have never seen him since. If they did find him, now, years later, they would probably find him in an alley somewhere, and he probably wouldn't even recognize his own parents because of the amount of drugs or chemicals in his system.

That's the person who comes to my mind when I think of someone who is 'failing' in every way. But in your own mind, think of an example of someone you know, or know of, who fits your picture of failure. Whoever it is, get a clear image of that person in your mind.

Then, imagine that person is also there with you right now, and is standing off to the left of you.

Now, in this experiment, you should have two people standing near you. On your right, there is the person who is succeeding in life. On your left is the person who is failing in life.

Take a moment, and examine each of them.

One of them—the successful one on the right—is living a life that works. Successful in every important way. Uplifting and fulfilling. Happy and feeling good about life.

The other person—the unsuccessful one on the left—is failing and spiraling downward. Unhappy and living a life that is not working.

Here's the key. This next question holds one of the most important answers to life itself:

Question: What is the *difference* between the two people—the one whose life is working, and the one whose life is not?

Answer: The difference between the two people is their *programs*.

It is their programs that caused them to live their lives in different ways—and created the success or failure each of them now has.

But the most important point is this: The two people you have imagined standing to your right and to your left—one of them so successful, and the other one failing at life—*those two people could have been the two infants we saw in the newborn nursery, that we looked in on just a short time ago.*

When they began their lives, they might have been the two little infants, just born, snuggled in their safe, warm, swaddling blankets in their little bassinets, their eyes wide open, searching, waiting to live out the unlimited potential they were each born to achieve.

And now, after time has passed, here they are, completely different in the outcome of their lives.

What is the difference? Why did each of them turn out the way they did?

The difference is their programs. When they were born, the opportunity to live a wonderful, fulfilling life was the same for each of them. But one of them ended up being wired to succeed. The other one ended up being wired to fail.

People who argue against this would tell you that it was life's challenges, its ups and downs that got in the way and changed the infant who failed. And they would say that it was good luck or fortune that interceded and made the successful person successful. Or they might say that it was just the difference in the two individuals' DNA.

But that's not the answer. The person who receives better, healthier, more positive programs will, over time, virtually always do better than the person who receives negative, unhealthy programs.

If you know someone who is doing really well, year after year, and continues to do so in spite of challenges—that's programs. If you know someone who is failing, time after time, continues to do so, and can't seem to get life right—that's programs.

It will be up to you to decide which of the program paths you choose to follow in your own life. Since you're reading this book, I can assume that you are one of the people who choose to be 'successful' at life. If you'd like to do that (or be even more successful than you already are), start with your programs. *Start with your self-talk.*

If any of your self-talk is inaccurate and negative, change it. Choose to reprogram your own brain with the right, positive self-talk, the right messages—the ones that should have been given to you in the first place.

Chapter Four

Negative Self-Talk Disorder

One of the most common behavioral problems people face today is the problem I have called *Negative Self-Talk Disorder*. The disorder has symptoms that can be identified, and it can be treated. But left unchecked, it can create catastrophic results.

The problem is that, while many people suffer from Negative Self-Talk Disorder, even though its effects are terribly damaging, most people are not aware they have it. Few of them have any understanding of the chaos negative self-talk is creating in their lives.

The following few questions will tell you if Negative Self-Talk Disorder may be a problem in your own life:

Do you often think negative thoughts?

Do you feel 'down' or depressed for no apparent reason?

Do you have trouble focusing on your goals and accomplishing the things you want to accomplish?

Do you argue more than you should?

Do you often feel that life is working against you?

Do you feel you are not in control of your future?

Do you put off or procrastinate doing the things you need to do?

Do you often see the worst first and the best last?

Do you talk about yourself in any way that puts you down or makes you think less of yourself?

Do you find that you are self-critical, and often critical of others?

Is a noticeable amount of your self-talk each day made up of negative thoughts?

Do you have trouble seeing the world, and life in general, as bright and as positive as you would like it to be?

Do you find that you have stopped believing in your dreams, and have started to believe that those dreams are no longer true for you?

If negative self-talk is playing a role in your life, you probably already see the results. People who are negative make themselves less capable at problem-solving than people who are more positive. They are unnecessarily unhappy—and they make themselves that way. They often have an inaccurately negative picture of the future. And, without knowing it, they afflict or affect everyone around them.

The problem is that Negative Self-Talk Disorder is an unconsciously acquired disorder that becomes physically, chemically, wired into your brain. (It becomes an actual disorder—faulty wiring—in the brain.) If you do nothing to change it, it not only stays, it also gets progressively worse. It becomes a part of your programs, and follows the rules under which your brain operates.

Imagine meeting a sour, pessimistic, down-in-the-mouth person who is negative about everything. When you meet someone like that, it is clear that person did not suddenly become a negative, unhappy person overnight.

People who are super-negative—whether they are aware of it or not—have worked at it. Probably for years. Day after day, thought after thought, they have, usually without knowing it, wired their brains to see the world in a darker, more insecure, less enlightened and optimistic way. If you ask them to look at the world in a bright and positive way, they can no longer do it. They're too negative. Their brains are now wired to be negative and to think that way, and that's how they see themselves and the world around them.

The 3 Levels of Negative Self-Talk Disorder

It is plain to see from the following brief overview that negative self-talk is not only a progressive disorder, but it is also a disorder which can grow to the point that it literally destroys lives.

Here are the symptoms of the three most recognizable levels of Negative Self-Talk Disorder:

Negative Self-Talk Disorder — Level 1

"The Beginner"

This is the person who is just beginning to wire his or her brain with more negative than positive. The problem may start with a single bad experience, or it may be the result of a series of difficult life circumstances. Or it may be the result of repeated negative programming from others. The result is a loss of belief in a positive outcome.

The Level 1 Person — Key Symptoms

Expresses frequent doubt.
Often feels depressed for no apparent reason.
Worries a lot.
Begins to feel a lack of control of life in general.
Expects (unrealistic) bad things to happen.
Begins to complain more often.

Smiles or laughs less often than usual.
Becomes self-critical and critical of others.
Shows signs of beginning to focus on the negative.
Begins to lose trust in things working out right.

Negative Self-Talk Disorder — Level 2

"The Practicing Downer"

Level 2 is the person who has practiced negative self-talk long enough for it to become that person's default way of looking at life. This person begins to miss life's opportunities by assuming the role of victim. They see the world as being unfair—to themselves in particular—and they are beginning to give up on anything wonderful or positive.

The Level 2 Person — Key Symptoms:

Is quick to point out what *won't* work.
Is often argumentative.
Stops being an active listener.
Often begins the day with a feeling of fatigue or dread.

Creates a cycle of self-induced depression.
Begins to be more focused on self than others.
May start to withdraw from social engagements.
Often sees problems as bigger than they are.
Is increasingly unable to see positive alternatives.
Becomes hyper-critical of others.
Becomes angry at outcomes.
Is seldom fun or uplifting to be around.
Frequently shows signs of doubting the future.
Increasingly feels a lack of control.
Often feels hopeless or discouraged.

Negative Self-Talk Disorder — Level 3

"The Graduate Negatroid"

This is the person who is negative about almost everything. This person has usually experienced long-term negative programming—often from childhood. They don't just have an occasional bad day; the Level 3 person doesn't know what a good day looks like. The Level 3 person does not live a happy and fulfilled life. Theirs is a life that is not working. A negative attitude and belief system surrounds almost everything the person thinks or believes.

The Level 3 Person — Key Symptoms:

Daily sees life from a negative point of view.
Has lost all trust in himself or herself and in others.
Has lost belief in things changing for the better.
Is seldom truly happy, and almost never smiles or laughs in a natural, genuinely happy way.
Is often selfish, and ignores the needs of others.
Lives with a daily attitude of criticism and doubt.
Believes positive thinking is wishful thinking, and criticizes others for being positive.
Believes that negative thinking is the realistic way to think.
Replaces hope with the acceptance of despair.
Replaces action with frustration and anger.
Is almost never fun or uplifting to be around.
Often forms deep facial stress and frown lines.
Adopts a fatalistic, 'losing' view of life.
Accepts failure as a natural outcome.
Usually ends up in an unhappy life that fails.

Because Negative Self-Talk Disorder is a progressive disorder, it usually starts gradually and, unless it is dealt with and reversed, it progresses to more and more unhealthy programs, until those programs, added together, become a way of life.

There is a reason why this happens. It starts with how the brain is wired.

Chapter Five

Negative Self-Talk and the Brain

The process by which the human brain creates, stores, and acts on your mental programs is somewhat complicated. I'll simplify the process here, to give you an overview of how it works.

(To read an in-depth look at self-talk and the brain, see my book, *The Power of Neuroplasticity*.)

The Neuroplasticity of Your Brain

Neuroplasticity refers to your brain's ability to form new neural networks and connections based on new input. This process takes place throughout your lifetime.

This means that your brain is always learning, and it is always changing. New learning or experience actually changes the physical structure—the wiring—of your brain.

Research into the brain's neuroplasticity has opened new doors of treatment for stroke victims, as well as people who struggle with dyslexia, learning disorders, and even brain damage.

The key here is that research in the field of neuroscience has identified the link between your thoughts and how your brain is wired. What you experience, what you think, and what you say, changes the synaptic connections in your brain.

And that means that what you have been thinking and saying—without being aware of it—has been wiring and changing your brain.

Your Brain Believes What it is Told Most

Deep inside the workings of the human brain, there is no actual '*truth*.' The part of the brain that stores all of the messages you have received, accepts what it is told most often. It then plays back to you the strongest messages it has received. And it plays those messages back to you as 'truth' or 'fact,' whether the messages are actually true or not.

That's why you can believe in one political ideology completely, when the other half of the population—many millions of people—believes in the opposite political ideology. And you, and all of them, think that your own beliefs are correct. (A perfect example of this is that many people, when voting, are actually voting based on their programmed biases, not on the actual qualifications of the candidate.)

What you believe about anything is not a measure of its correctness. What you believe about anything is a measure of the programs you have that support your belief.

Just as with your political beliefs, your brain has stored an immense number of programs about you—everything you believe to be true about you.

However, what your brain has collected and stored about you may not really be true at all; it is just the sum total of the programs you have received about you—both from the outside world, and from your own self-talk. A lot of those programs may be wrong. Maybe most of them.

If enough of your programs are negative, your self-talk will also be negative. *Your self-talk is the result of the programs you have that are the strongest.* (Negative programs = negative self-talk.)

Neuroplasticity and Repetition in the Brain

We have learned from the field of neuroscience that because of the brain's neuroplasticity—its ability to continue to change itself throughout your lifetime––the most important chemical process necessary to wiring or rewiring your brain is *repetition*. The brain is designed to pay attention to, and store, the messages that are repeated most often.

A message your brain receives only once will be stored in your brain's short-term memory only briefly. It doesn't become 'wired in' to your brain's long-term storage files.

34

But when that same message is repeated frequently, usually over time, your brain begins to form new neural connections. It wires the new message into, and connects it with, the vast neural networks of your conscious and unconscious mind.

It is because the brain stores messages that are *repeated*, that we end up believing what we believe about most everything—as we just saw in the example of why we believe in the politics we follow.

It is also because the brain stores—and wires in— repeated messages, that *you end up believing things about you that you tell yourself most often*. The complete 'you' that you believe you are today, is the combined result of years of messages, both from the world around you and, most importantly, from your own self-talk.

Whatever messages you got from the world you live in, combined with what your experiences have caused you to say to yourself in your own self-talk, have created everything you believe to be true about yourself today.

Some of the messages your brain received about you may have been true. But many other messages your brain received were not true at all!

And together, those messages, through repetition, have created what you believe about yourself. Your life, all of your opinions, and everything you believe about who you are today, is the result of the repetition of messages to your brain.

If the programming of the brain is based on repetition, and if your own self-talk is negative, what is the only outcome you can predict?

Remember: we continually repeat and replay the programs we get most often. And the strongest program always wins. The key to failure is the repetition of a belief in failure. Negative self-talk is the repetition of a belief in failure.

Your Prefrontal Cortex

At one time, skeptics believed that "positive thinking" was nothing more than wishful thinking, and that the idea of positive thinking was something you could read about in a self-help book—but it wouldn't really make your life any better.

However, subsequent brain research has shown an entirely different story: People who have trained their brains to think in the *positive,* actually wire more neural networks into the *left* prefrontal cortex of their brain. That's a part of the brain that helps you seek options and alternatives, *helps you find a better way to deal with the problem,* and puts you into positive action.

And what about negative self-talkers? People who habitually think in the *negative,* wire more neural networks into the *right* prefrontal cortex of their brains. That's a part of the brain that causes you to *shut down your options* and get the heck out of there. It puts you into escape mode, fight or flight mode, and stops you from taking the action you should be taking.

Negative Self-Talk and Your Subconscious Mind

Your subconscious mind makes most of your choices for you—without you being aware of it.

That's kind of scary, because as much as 90% or more of your mental programs are hidden from you; they are buried in your subconscious mind. It is safe to say that you have virtually tens of thousands of programs that are directing your life right now, and you are not actually aware of what most of those programs are.

I mentioned earlier that in the average individual, 77% or more of their unconscious programs are negative. This means that not only is your subconscious mind silently making most of your choices for you, but it is also making those choices based on programs that are mostly *negative*.

When a family member calls unexpectedly, what is the first thought that comes to your mind? Do you automatically think 'good news,' or do you immediately fear 'bad news?' When you're about to step on the scale to see what you weigh, what do you think first? When you hear that someone has said something about you on social media, what thought is going through your mind as you go online to read it for yourself?

Your thoughts—thousands of them each day—are controlled by the programs you have spent years storing in your subconscious mind.

If you program the navigational computer on an airplane to fly in a particular direction, that is the direction the airplane will fly—*even if it's the wrong direction*. If you program the directional computer of your own brain to send your thoughts and your actions in the wrong direction, that is the direction your thoughts and your actions will be programmed to go—even if it's the wrong direction.

The obvious solution to this problem would be to get rid of the mental programs you have that are negative, and to make sure you have enough positive programs stored in your subconscious mind to ensure that your attitudes and actions will also be positive.

But the dilemma has been, how do you get rid of negative programs when they are hidden—when they are buried deep in your subconscious mind, and you don't even know what they are?

How do you fix the problem of negative self-talk, and the negative programs it creates?

Chapter Six

Fixing the Problem of Negative Self-Talk

Many years ago, when I first began to recognize the truth about negative self-talk and how it destroys lives, I made two life-changing decisions.

The first was that I would never again give in to negative programming, of any kind, in my own life, if I could help it in any way.

The second decision I made in this area was that I would research the concept of self-talk and programming, and explore the science behind the concept.

The result of my first decision was that I stopped, ever again, using negative self-talk in my own life. The result of the second decision, to do serious research into the concept of self-talk, took more than thirty years, and resulted in my writing more than twenty books on the subject.

I discussed earlier how negative self-talk and the programming of the human brain works. But it's equally important to know what to *do* about the problem.

If you have negative programs now, can they be changed? Can you create new, more positive programs in the brain? And most important, what specific steps can you follow to get rid of old negative programs—and, at the same time, create positive new programs?

My research into the neuroscience behind self-talk uncovered important answers. Not only did I discover how we get programmed, and how destructive most of that programming is, a lot of what I found gave us the answers that would tell us how to fix the problem.

I'll summarize the answers I found:

1. Can you erase the negative programs you have now?

Even if you have programs that have been wired into your brain for years, you can change or reverse them. If you do nothing, they are usually 'permanent.' If you have any level of Negative Self-Talk Disorder, and you do nothing to change it, it will get worse. However, if you replace the old negative programs with positive new programs, you can override the negative ones.

Important Note #1: Even if some of your negative programs have been with you for years—perhaps a lifetime—because of the brain's plasticity, it does *not* take years to erase or replace them. Replacing negative programs often takes only weeks, not years.

Important Note #2: You don't have to identify every single negative program you have now, in order to erase it or replace it. The recommendations you'll find here will help you override negative programs, even if they are completely hidden in your subconscious mind.

2. Can you create entirely new, more positive programs?

Yes. Since you got your current programs through repetition, you can create new programs in the same way. By using repetition, *you can create any new program you choose.*

3. What are the steps to creating new programs?

'How to change your programs' has been the subject of several of my previous books. (Most notably, see the book, *What to Say When You Talk to Your Self.*)

To simplify the process for you here, and break it down to its basic steps, I have included the following guide to changing your self-talk, which was formulated by the Self-Talk Institute.

The Self-Talk Institute was founded in 1985, and has spent over three decades researching negative self-talk and brain programming, as well as conducting seminars on positive self-talk methods and techniques, and also training certified self-talk

44

trainers. From its decades of experience in helping many thousands of individuals successfully change their self-talk, the Institute has identified the most effective methods for doing this.

When I'm speaking to an audience, or when I'm being interviewed for a blog or a media appearance, the guidelines I use are from the Self-Talk Institute. They are well-researched and solid. They are the best guidelines we have found for people who want to change their programs, and want to get it right.

The following guide is made up of two parts. The first part includes the specific steps you need to take to change your self-talk. The second part consists of a quiz that will identify the areas of your self-talk that you may want to change.

Here is the Self-Talk Institute's guide:

THE SELF-TALK INSTITUTE
Guide to Changing Your Self-Talk

The purpose of this guide is to give the reader the most effective and practical methods available to create the habit of positive self-talk, and overcome the damaging effects of negative self-talk.

Many thousands of once-negative self-talkers have followed these steps, and have changed both their self-talk and their lives as a result.

A word of encouragement: Your brain is designed to change. It is designed to *rewire* itself with new input. When you practice or listen to positive new self-talk, your brain will begin to erase the old negative neural programs naturally, pruning out the old programs and making space for the new. If you follow the steps below, and stay with it, it will work.

The Three Steps

There are three primary steps to changing your self-talk from negative to positive:

46

Step 1: *Monitor*

As you're getting started, for the next 30 days, monitor your self-talk as it is now. Listen to everything you think, and everything you say.

Imagine having someone record everything you said for 30 days. Then, at the end of that time, they transcribed your words and typed them out, and then underlined with a yellow highlighter everything you had said most often.

If you were to read a list of those highlighted phrases, you would have an accurate picture of your self-talk as it is today. It would not include the self-talk you thought silently to yourself each day, but it would give you a clear picture of what your spoken self-talk sounds like right now.

What is the first thing you usually say to greet each day?

What goes through your mind when the traffic light turns red?

How do you react when your child comes home with a bad grade?

What goes through your mind when someone disagrees with you?

What is the last thing you think before you go to sleep at night?

Even without actually writing down your self-talk, the goal is to become consciously aware of all of your thoughts and all of your words. When you start focusing on your current self-talk every day, you will begin to recognize the self-talk you are using now that could be working against you.

The purpose of creating the habit of monitoring your self-talk is to become *mindful*. Becoming consciously mindful of your self-talk is the first step in changing it.

Step 2: *Edit*

Each time you catch yourself saying or thinking anything that is harmfully negative, do the following: *Stop–* –and *restate* it in the *positive*.

As an example, imagine that you've just made a mistake, and you hear yourself saying something like, *"I'm so stupid."* Immediately replace it with, *"That's not like me. I'm smarter than that."* Or, when you hear yourself about to say, *"Nothing ever works out right for me,"* replace the negative with a clear, new positive directive to your brain: *"I am good at making things work. I have a plan, I follow it, I stay with it, and I achieve my goal."*

As you can see, the negatives in those examples are replaced with clear, positive statements that give new directives to your brain.

When you edit your self-talk in this way, you're not lying to yourself by replacing the negative thought with positive; you're rewiring your brain with an accurate picture of how you *choose* to be—the new picture of you that you're now creating. You're not kidding yourself; you're setting the record straight.

Learning to edit your thoughts and your words is an essential step, but it doesn't get rid of all of the old negative programs you have stored up. Editing will, however, help protect you from getting more of them.

As a technique used by itself, editing won't teach you a refreshing new language of optimism and success, but it can help stop the old negative language from getting stronger.

Step 3: *Listen to Self-Talk*

Today, when you want to learn a new language, the most effective way to learn that language is by listening to recorded sessions of the language, and then practicing it. Learning the language of positive self-talk works the same way. The easiest and most effective way to learn self-talk is by listening to it.

Learning the New Language of Positive Self-Talk

In the brain, learning positive self-talk utilizes the same process as learning a new language—through repeated listening, and then practicing what you're learning.

Repetition is the key. When you listen to positive self-talk—about 10 to 15 minutes each day—you will be giving clear, positive, new messages to your brain. Because of the daily repetition, your brain will begin to override and replace the older, negative self-talk programs which had been dominant.

You can expect to see early, positive changes in your attitude and motivation even in the first days of listening. However, it typically takes about three weeks or more for the brain to begin to rewire itself with new, repeated programs, so set a goal to stay with it.

As you begin learning and practicing the new self-talk, you will also begin to wire in the habit of changing your programs naturally—both consciously and unconsciously. *That's the turning point you're looking for.*

Because you're hearing and practicing self-talk each day, the new self-talk will become the new language you think in and speak in naturally. It is that new language—a new way of dealing with life—that will begin to inform every future choice you make.

Note: When you listen to self-talk, it is recommended that you play the sessions primarily in the background, while you are doing something else, and do not try to focus on them. Your brain will be listening, whether you are consciously listening or not. In this way, you will be less likely to question the positive new programs while your brain is going through the process of wiring them in.

The Self-Talk Institute offers an online streaming service, called SelfTalkPlus.com. This service allows you to listen to self-talk programs on a broad variety of topics that affect your life, both personally and professionally. With the Institute's streaming service, you can listen to positive self-talk programs on your phone or on any listening device. The service is free for the first 30 days, and is open to all users. To access this service, go to www.SelfTalkPlus.com.

The Self-Talk Quiz

Whether you work at changing your self-talk on your own, or participate in the Self-Talk Institute's online listening program, the following quiz will help you identify which areas of your self-talk require your attention, and which areas you should work on first.

When you take this quiz, be honest. It is important that you know which areas of your self-talk are working for you, and which areas may be working against you.

In the following quiz, rate each of the questions from *1* to *10.*

A high score of *8, 9* or *10* means your self-talk in that subject area is positive, and is working *for* you.

If you score yourself a *5, 6,* or *7,* it tells you that those areas may need work, even if they aren't your first priority.

A score of *1* to *4* means your self-talk in that area needs immediate attention. (The lower the score, the more your self-talk in that area needs help.)

Rate your typical self-talk in each of the following areas:

1. *Your Self-Esteem*
How do you generally feel about yourself as an individual, overall?

Rate your self-talk about your self-esteem: _____

2. *Being in Control of Your Life*
Are you on top, in control of your life, and going for it? What is your self-talk when you think or talk about being in control?

Rate your self-talk about how much you feel you're in control of your life: _____

3. *Your Health and Fitness*
When you talk about, or think about, your level of health and fitness, how do you usually describe yourself?

Rate your self-talk about health and fitness: _____

4. *Your Job or Career*
Do you always praise your job and your work—or does your self-talk say something else?

Rate your self-talk about your job or career: _____

5. *Money and Finances*
What are the messages you give yourself most about money—and how easy it is for you to attain financial freedom?

Rate your self-talk about money and finances: _____

6. *Your Relationships*
Do you automatically and naturally see your relationships working as you would like them to, or do you feel you could improve them in some areas?

Rate your self-talk about your relationships: _____

7. *The Quality of Your Life*
Is your life working each day at its highest, most fulfilling level? Or would you like it to be better?

Rate your self-talk about the quality of your life: _____

8. *Reaching Your Goals*
Do your thoughts and your self-talk show a picture of you reaching all of your goals?

Rate your self-talk about how you're doing at reaching your goals: _____

9. *Getting Things Done*
Does your self-talk tell you that you are accomplishing everything you would like to—on time, and in the right way? Is procrastination a problem for you?

Rate your self-talk about your success in getting things done: _____

10. *Your Appearance*
Does your self-talk tell you that you are happy with your appearance, and looking your best?

Rate your self-talk about your appearance: _____

11. *Your Weight*
What does your self-talk tell you about your weight, and how you feel about it? What kind of self-talk do you use when you think about your weight?

Rate your self-talk about your weight: _____

12. *Your Attitude*
When you monitor your self-talk, what does it tell you about your attitude? Is it positive, and as good as you would like it to be?

Rate your self-talk that reflects your attitude overall: _____

13. *How You Deal With Problems*
Does your self-talk describe you as being on top of your game, and always dealing with problems well?
Rate your self-talk about dealing with problems: _____

14. *Your Intelligence*
Does your self-talk tell you that you are confident about your intelligence?

Rate your self-talk about how you feel about your intelligence: _____

15. *Your Energy*
When you talk about your energy, do you see yourself as having a lot of energy, or do you tell yourself you never have enough?
Rate your self-talk about your level of energy: _____

16. *Your Stress*
Does your self-talk show a picture of you that is relaxed, calm, and in control, or does it show you that you have too much stress in your life?

Rate your self-talk about your stress and your daily sense of calm: _____

17. *Anxiety or Depression*
Does your self-talk show a picture of you that is positive and upbeat, or frequently 'down,' anxious or depressed?

Rate your self-talk about feeling anxious or depressed:

_____

18. *Being Organized*
When you think—or talk about—how organized you feel you are, does your self-talk say you are as organized as you would like to be?

Rate your self-talk each day about being organized, and feeling you're on top of things: _____

19. *Your Sense of 'Purpose' in Life*
What do you say about your purpose or your mission in life? Is your purpose crystal clear, or do you need more clarity in this area?

Rate your self-talk about having a sense of purpose in your life: _____

20. *Looking Forward to Tomorrow*
Does your self-talk give you an uplifting and positive picture of your future?

Rate your self-talk about looking forward to your future:

_____

21. *Your Personal Growth*

Does your self-talk show you a picture of you that is always growing and improving?

Rate your self-talk about how you are growing as an individual: _____

* * * * *

Carefully examining your scores on the above quiz will tell you where to start, and which areas of your self-talk you need to work on most.

Take a moment now and make a note of your three lowest score areas. This will tell you where to begin, as you start working to change your old programs.

Note: If you listen to self-talk sessions, about 10 to 15 minutes a day as recommended by The Self-Talk Institute, plan to retake the above quiz again 90 days from now. You may be surprised how dramatically your scores change for the better, even in that short period of time.

Guide to Changing Your Self-Talk™
© 2019 The Self-Talk Institute.

The above guide from The Self-Talk Institute has been very successful at helping many thousands of individuals change their self-talk. If you would like to put yourself on the fast track to having the right self-talk in your life, I encourage you to follow their guidelines.

It is easy to see, from the above quiz, how many areas of your life are being directly affected every day by the self-talk you have now. You cannot help but consider the question:

"What would happen if you made the choice to improve your self-talk in *all* the key areas of your life?"

Chapter Seven

Changing Your Self-Talk

Until people have heard the specific kind of of self-talk that most rapidly creates positive changes, they often struggle with what form it should take, and what it should sound like.

Here is an example of correctly-worded self-talk, taken from one of my favorite recorded self-talk sessions. This one is on the subject of Self-Esteem:

You like yourself. You choose to like who you are. You feel good about yourself. You like the way you think. You like the things you do. You like the way you live your life. You have self-confidence. You know yourself, and you are proud of the person you have chosen to be. An accurate description of you would include the words, "wonderful, unique, well-liked, positive, self-directed, happy, and incredible."

You are a quality person. You are worthwhile. You deserve to live at your best, and to receive the best from the life you live. You attract the best in everything around you. People really enjoy your company. They like the way you think. They like the way you express yourself. And they like the person you are.

You really deserve good things in your life. Each morning, you wake up feeling good about yourself. You are happy with the way you see yourself each day. You are proud of the job you're doing, making your life count.

The self-talk messages above are written in 'second person'—to you, from your 'internal coach'—who is showing you at your best.

Positive self-talk messages are also used extensively in 'first person,' as in, *"I am . . ."*

The Self-Talk Institute recommends using both forms when practicing or listening to self-talk.

Stated in first person, the messages are from 'you' to 'you,' as you take control of redefining who you are, and how you choose to be:

I build self-esteem every day. I talk to myself, and in just the right way. I always do everything it takes to make sure that my self-esteem is strong, positive, and working for me in the best possible way.

I never put myself down. I always build myself up. I have strong, positive pride in who I am. I let other people know it, and I let myself know it. I stand tall. I think sharp. I look good. And I am in control of my life, and I like who I am. That's me. That's who I choose to be.

I allow nothing to stand between me and my most positive self-esteem. Every morning when I awake, I make the conscious choice to feel good about myself all day. I have learned to say the words of self-talk which tell me, "I like myself. I'm glad to be me. Today is my day."

Imagine your own brain receiving those kinds of messages every day—with enough repetition to wire them in as absolute truths about you! They bring to life the person you were born to be in the first place.

When your brain receives repeated messages like those—messages that redefine how you feel about yourself and your place in this world—your brain begins to record them and keep them. They are like the words to a song that changes your life, and never leaves you.

In the recorded format the above messages are taken from, each of the self-talk phrases is repeated three separate times, with different word emphasis and intonation in each repetition. There is a reason for this:

The combination of *wording, repetition* and *emphasis* increases the amount of neural networks that are being formed and activated in your brain—which increases the *strength* of the program message you're receiving. That creates stronger programming in the brain. Multiply that effect over dozens of additional, correct self-talk phrases, and you can easily see why the new self-talk is able to overpower and replace the old.

In Your Brain, Positive Self-Talk is Contagious

When you begin to actively change your self-talk in one area of your life, don't be surprised if your self-talk in other areas also begins to improve.

This is because when you change your self-talk and create new programs in one area, your brain will automatically begin to form new neural networks in other *similar* or complementary areas.

For instance, you may choose to listen to self-talk to lose weight, and suddenly find yourself getting more organized. Or, you may listen to self-talk sessions to improve your relationships, and discover that you are also improving your self-esteem.

When you begin working on the areas of your self-talk that are the most important to you, other areas of your brain will begin to get in tune, and duplicate the same kind of positive activity.

Start with the self-talk you want to work on most, and stay with it. When you do, additional areas of your self-talk will begin to follow.

63

Choosing to Change Your Self-Talk
Is an Important Choice

I could not imagine waking up in the morning and saying, *"It's going to be another one of those days,"* or *"It's another blue Monday."* When I face a problem, and I've had to face many, as all of us do, I never find myself saying, *"I can't deal with this!"* The thought never enters my mind.

It's not, in any way, that I think I'm special. It's that I made the choice to change my self-talk. I first practiced self-talk by listening to it. I wanted to lose weight, and, incredibly, I lost 58 pounds in the process. (And I kept if off.) I then began listening to and practicing self-talk in many other areas, until it became a natural part of my life.

The result is, to me, a rainy day is not a bad day. A skinned knee is not a fatal event. A negative remark from someone is not the end of the world. And a bad day is not the most important day of my life.

How you think about each of those kinds of things is a choice—one of *hundreds* of choices you make every day. But you can only make the best choices when the majority of your mental programs are aligned with a primary, underlying choice—*to deal with life in a positive way.*

It seems like such a simple thing, that one small choice: *"I choose to change my self-talk. I choose to deal with life in a positive way."* But it is one of the most important choices you can ever make. It is profound. It is life-changing.

The problem is that deciding to look at life that way is one thing. Actually *doing* it is another. If you do nothing to support your new goal, what happens next is almost entirely controlled by the old programs you already have that may see your life differently.

That's why you can get motivated and excited by a good idea—like setting a goal to start going to the gym, or a goal to start a new diet—and then, a week or two later, the idea is gone. You're back to your old self. You're no longer working out, or you're no longer on your diet. *What happened?*

What happened is, your old programs stepped in and took over once again. Which is exactly what your old programs are designed to do.

If many of your hidden, subconscious programs are negative, disbelieving, or working against you, what else can you expect? Whether you believe you are or not, you may not be as in control of your life as you think you are.

Unless you choose to take control of your own mental programming process, the result is inevitable: the programs you have now are controlling you. Not the other way around.

But if you choose to change your self-talk—and make the commitment to stay with it long enough to create a new self-talk habit—then that habit, itself, will become wired into your brain. Once that happens, your own brain will begin to motivate you to continue. When you reach that point, life begins to change. You will personally be in control.

Chapter Eight

Key Questions and Their Answers

This chapter identifies the most frequently asked questions about negative self-talk and includes my personal answers to each of them.

I have studied and taught the concept of self-talk for most of my professional career, now over 40 years. In that time, I have also had the honor of speaking to hundreds of audiences, often made up of many thousands of attendees. My favorite part of any speaking event is the question and answer period. And I doubt there is any question on this subject that I haven't been asked.

Here are what I believe to be the most important questions about negative self-talk, and their answers.

1. *Can anyone change their self-talk?*

If you want to change your self-talk, you can. I've never met anyone who wanted to change their self-talk who couldn't do it. In most cases, they had wanted to change it, and they had to follow a few practical steps, as outlined in the Institute's guide. But when they followed those steps, their self-talk changed.

The reason people achieve reliable success with this is that the brain is *designed* to rewire itself. So, if you learn how to rewire your brain in the right way, your brain has no choice. It will do what it was designed to do. The key is to make your brain's natural programming process work *for* you instead of against you.

2. How long does it take to change your self-talk if you're actively working at it?

If you're on the fast track, following the Institute's recommendations and listening to positive self-talk audio sessions daily, you will notice a difference in your thinking almost immediately, within the first few days. That will tell you it's starting to work.

As was stated in the guide, it takes a minimum of three to four weeks of repetition for the new self-talk to start actually becoming *wired in*. However, you'll notice the differences in your self-talk—and in your thinking—even while that's happening. Then, by staying with it, your new self-talk will continue to get stronger and stronger, until *thinking* in the new self-talk becomes a fully wired-in habit.

3. When should you start teaching positive self-talk to kids?

Start being a self-talk role model now, whatever age your kids are. Any child or young person above the age of about two years old begins to understand the idea of repeated messages.

Most kids today, from about age four or five on up, are familiar with computers or personal electronic devices, and can understand that what you type into them is what you get back out.

Always let them know you believe in them. And then, talk to them about their own self-talk, and let them know that whatever they tell their own mental computer is what they will get back. Self-belief and self-determination have created more great kids than almost anything else.

Remember, *you* are the most important programmer your kids will ever have.

4. Can you change your self-talk by writing 'affirmations' or reminders, and reading them to yourself each day? Or do you need to listen to new self-talk to replace the old?

Affirmations, for the most part, are good. The problem is that, in their common use today, affirmations are seldom strong enough, or detailed enough, to change your underlying programs. Without the right strength and specific detail, reading or repeating a few affirmations each day will not change the programs that are buried in the subconscious part of your brain.

The popular use of affirmations was one of the starting gates into my research into self-talk. What I found is that, while many affirmations express wonderful sentiments like *"I am one with the divine* universe," or *"The world gives to me what I declare,"* the words can make you feel better for a short time, but the affirmations themselves do almost nothing to rewire your brain.

Most affirmations, as they are used today, are not worded in a way that your brain can interpret them as actual, specific directions that you want it to follow. And that's the problem: Affirmations don't pay the rent, or get you to work on time.

I have occasionally been challenged for suggesting that people should listen to recorded self-talk instead of doing something more 'homemade' or personal, such as writing self-talk refrigerator notes or putting affirmations on the mirror. But changing your brain takes more than that.

*   *   *   *   *

Over the years, I've gone through all of the easy-sounding steps for changing a person's internal self-talk from negative to positive. But it gets down to

71

physics, the chemistry of the brain, and how rewiring the brain actually works.

Knowing the science and the truth of that, if I had only one chance to help anyone I cared about change their self-talk and get it right—based on what neuroscience and many years of experience have taught me—I would urge them to listen to self-talk recordings every day.

5. How does self-talk relate to spiritual beliefs?

The concept of changing your self-talk, because it is based on solid neuroscience, is accepted broadly, worldwide, and it is understood and used daily by people of all faiths.

The Bible itself (where I was first introduced to the idea of changing your self-talk), written centuries before modern technology, speaks directly to the importance of changing your thoughts in Romans 12:2 when it says, "*. . . be transformed by the renewing of your mind.*" That is one of my favorite verses in the Bible. And that's exactly what the right self-talk helps you do. Imagine being transformed, by the renewing of your mind! It is a thought that has never left me.

6. Can you change someone else's negative self-talk if they don't know they have a problem, or if they don't want to change their own self-talk?

With most adults, the short answer is 'No.' If the other person isn't interested in changing, they probably won't.

The most frequent exception to this is when a husband or a wife, for example, has wanted to help their mate change his or her self-talk from negative to positive.

In each case, the helpful partner played audio self-talk sessions in the background each morning, while the two of them were getting ready for work, without mentioning to their partner that the intent was to help them.

Over time, usually a few weeks, the negative partner began to show a difference in attitude, and then began rephrasing comments into a positive form.

Once they became aware that their thinking was improving, they began to make noticeable, and often life-changing, improvements. This is another case where their brain was listening, and taking the self-talk in, even if they weren't *actively* listening.

This 'eavesdrop' method can also work well with teenagers and younger kids.

7. What if you don't believe it will work?

What if you ignore the science, or don't accept the concept, or just don't believe changing your self-talk will work?

The answer is that your brain doesn't care whether you believe it or not. If you change the repeated messages you give to your brain, it will record them, wire them in, and act on them. It has no choice.

8. How can you protect yourself from the negative self-talk of others?

In your brain, the strongest programs win. That means that if you have strong, positive programs yourself, you will be less likely to be influenced by the negative programs of people around you, or other input sources like today's often negative internet posts, and even television news.

You can't change the world's negative programs, but you can make sure that the programs *you* have are very strong and very positive. When you do that, your stronger, more positive programs will override the negatives you hear from others.

Don't be surprised, however, that when you start practicing self-talk, you may find yourself making changes like being more careful in selecting the people you choose to spend your time with, limiting the time you spend reading toxic posts online, or notice yourself watching fewer programs on television that focus on bad news.

9. How important is it to know what your negative programs are, or how you got them?

We've learned that it's best if you spend almost no time focusing on every negative program you might have, or how you got each of them. Other than monitoring your programs now, so you can get a clear picture of what they are, the more you focus on old negative programs, the more you will send new energy to them and make them stronger.

(An exception to this is exploring old, deeply-rooted programs with a therapist or counselor who understands self-talk and programming.)

Instead of spending time focusing on your old, negative programs, focus instead on a new decision to learn and practice the new language of positive self-talk. Then, stick with it. In time, the new programs will replace the old.

10. Are there any drawbacks to listening to self-talk or starting to think in the positive?

Yes. As an example, when you begin to seriously think better, or differently—in the positive—you could lose some of your 'friends' (that is, the negative people who weren't your real friends in the first place).

You could find yourself making a change in your career path.

You may no longer be comfortable about going nowhere in some areas of your life and choose to make some changes in those areas. That can create some dramatic changes you have to deal with.

You may start setting new goals in your life that could surprise everyone you know.

Those kinds of situations may appear to be drawbacks at first, but they usually turn out to be positive changes, as the new self-talk begins to go to work in your life.

11. What are the primary benefits of changing your self-talk?

Turning your life from thinking negative to living positive by changing your self-talk has a long list of benefits. Here are just a few of them:

a. You like yourself more, and you also care about others more.

b. You change from living in fear of tomorrow to living with positive, but realistic, anticipation for the exciting things tomorrow can bring.

c. People who think positively, both about their life, and about themselves as individuals, tend to get more organized and more in control of their life each day.

d. People who change their self-talk to the positive often begin taking care of themselves more, and as a result, live a more healthy life, overall.

e. In nearly every case, people who change their self-talk report that their relationships almost immediately begin to get better. Their honesty is more intact, and they are able to deal with the normal challenges with other people in a more direct, positive, and effective way. (When one of you stops being negative, it stops the negative cycle—and that can't help but improve the relationship.)

f. People who change their self-talk set goals that are more clearly defined, and then take the right steps to reach them—sometimes, for the first time ever.

g. People who practice positive self-talk typically find that they reduce stress in their life, and create more peace of mind.

h. Changing your self-talk improves your quality of life. You see things in a brighter, more optimistic way, and you are able to deal with problems more effectively.

i. Focusing on positive self-talk in specific areas of your life can help you achieve benefits such as losing weight, doing better at your job, getting clear on your career focus, improving your relationship with your partner, getting along better with your kids, increasing your income, finding your purpose in life . . . or all of the above.

12. What stops some people from changing their self-talk?

When the results of changing your self-talk are apparent, clearly helpful, and usually life-changing, why would anyone who understands the idea not immediately embark on a program to change their self-talk? What stops them?

Their old programs stop them.

Procrastination, fear, doubt, disbelief, and *denial* are the tools of self-sabotage that keep us from doing what we know we should do. And all of these are *programs.*

Surprisingly, it is technology that is helping people get past their excuses. Because of our current technology—with smartphones and tablets—we have an easier way to learn the language of positive self-talk.

Today, changing your self-talk requires only that you click on a "play" symbol on your favorite topic on the online self-talk streaming site, and let the new self-talk play in the background as you go about your day. When you do that, you are suddenly listening to the exact self-talk that overrides the negative programs that caused the procrastination, the fear, the doubt, the disbelief, and the denial in the first place.

When this happens, and you begin to experience the results for yourself, it may seem like magic, but it isn't. It's a combination of neuroscience, technology, and your own desire to change your self-talk for the better.

Chapter Nine

My Hope for You

There you have it. That, in as few words as I could pare it down to, is how self-talk works—and the best ways we have found to get rid of negative self-talk forever.

Having studied this subject, perhaps in more detail than anyone living today, and also having watched the positive progress of the new kind of self-talk in the lives of so many people, I am certain of this: when you change your self-talk, you change your life.

When you make the choice to change your self-talk, you actively reclaim the promise of the unlimited potential that you were given when you were first born.

Changing your self-talk is something virtually anyone can do. And the process starts with one small, but incredibly important step. Make the decision to begin with one of the most important phrases of self-talk you could ever say:

"I choose to change my self-talk."

That statement—that commitment to your future —can make all the difference in the world.

You Were the Infant in the Bassinet

It isn't possible for you to remember the first few days of your life. But at one time, you were that infant in the newborn nursery, snuggled into your little infant bassinet, your eyes wide open, searching for your unlimited future. In that amazing moment, you had your entire life in front of you.

Always remember: you NEVER LOSE the incredible promise and potential you were born with. EVER. You never lose it; it just gets buried under the programs you have that are covering it up—but it's still there.

Right now, wherever you are in your life, you still have every bit of that promise and that potential within you. *And you still have the rest of your life in front of you.*

With what we have learned about the human brain and how it can change—by the blessing of your birth, you have been given a wonderful gift. It is the gift that tells you an amazing truth about yourself:

You no longer have to live with negative self-talk. If you want to change your programs, you can.

Monitor, edit, listen, and *practice.* And don't stop. My hope for you is that you do exactly that.

There is no greater path you can walk,
no greater goal you can achieve,
and no greater purpose you can find,
than to live up to the promise
you were born to fulfill.

84

To contact Dr. Shad Helmstetter, or to arrange for his appearance on interviews or blogs:

Email — shadhelmstetteroffice@gmail.com

Other books by Shad Helmstetter

What to Say When You Talk to Your Self
The Power of Neuroplasticity
365 Days of Positive Self-Talk
365 Days of Positive Self-Talk for Weight-Loss
365 Days of Positive Self-Talk for Finding Your Purpose
The Boy Who Wanted to Change the World
    (an autobiography)

Children's Books:
The Incredible Adventure of Shadrack the Self-Talk Bear — Book One — The Story of Planet Excellence

The Incredible Adventure of Shadrack the Self-Talk Bear — Book Two — The Incredibears on Planet Earth

The Incredible Adventure of Shadrack the Self-Talk Bear — Book Three — The Rise of The Great Bear

The Incredible Adventure of Shadrack the Self-Talk Bear — Book Four — Doomsday on Planet Earth

Made in the
USA
Monee, IL